1. Introduction

Suicide is commended as an escape from the ills of life, and riches are to be despised. Aelian's Stoicism hardly goes below the surface. His primary object is to entertain and while so doing to convey instruction in the most agreeable form.

He was among the first to break away from the age-long tradition of the periodic structure of sentences, at least for works of a serious nature, and to affect a simpler prose of short, coordinated, sometimes paratactic, clauses.

In this and in the rich variety of topics and in a certain fondness for piquant, not to say earthy, stories from the life of men and of animals one may trace the influence of the Milesian Tales.

Unfettered by any canons of style or language, picaresque, and sometimes gross, they pandered to popular taste. To adopt their technique while refining the style and imparting a moral flavour to his narratives may well have seemed to Aelian a sure way of gaining a like popularity with educated readers.

Some might find fault with his random and piece-meal handling of his theme-of that he is well aware, and in the Epilogue he defends himself with the plea that a frequent change of topic helps to maintain the reader's interest and saves him from boredom.

But as to the permanent value of his work he has no misgivings, and since. Philostratus informs us that his writings were much admired, we may assume that they appealed to cultivated circles in a way that the voluminous and possibly arid compilations of grammarians did not.

2. The ibex of Libya

The Wild Goats which tread the mountain heights of Libya are about the size of oxen, but their thighs, breasts, and necks are covered with long and very shaggy hair, and so too are their jaws. Their foreheads are curved and rounded; their eyes are yellow, and their legs stumpy.

Their horns united at the beginning, part asunder and grow aslant: for they are not straight like those of other mountain goats but turn downwards obliquely and extend as far as the shoulders. Consequently they are of considerable length.

And these Goats spring with ease from towering pinnacles — ' crags ' as pastoral and poetical folk like to call them — on to another, height, for they are far better at leaping than all other kinds of goat. If, however, one should happen to fall owing to the spot which should receive it being beyond its reach, it has such a reserve of strength in its limbs that it remains uninjured on landing: At any rate not a thing does it break, even though it falls down a cleft rock, neither horn nor front of the skull.

But these creatures are as strong and as resistant as the stone itself. Now it is on the actual ridges that most of them are caught, by means of nets, spears, and snares, and by the general skill of a huntsman, but especially by skill in hunting the Goat. They are also caught in the plains, and there they cannot run strongly enough to escape. So even a man who is slow of foot will take them. And it seems; that their hide and horns are serviceable.

Thus, in the severest winters their hide keeps out the cold for' herdsmen and woodcutters, while those famous horns of theirs are useful in summer time for drawing water and drinking from a flowing stream or some bubbling spring and help to quench thirst, for they allow you to drink at one draught not a drop less than the contents of the largest cups, until you hay& cooled your panting heat and quenched all the fire and flame:

And so if: the inside is cleaned out by; some skilled polisher of horns, either horn will easily contain as much as three measures.

3. The Tortoise of Libya

Tortoises too are a product of Libya; they have a most cruel look, and they live in the mountains, and their shell is good for making lyres.

4. Mares-frenzy

When a Mare gives birth, some say that a small piece of flesh is attached to the foal's forehead, others say to its loin, others again to its genitals. This piece the Mare bites off and destroys; and it is called 'Mares-frenzy.

It is because Nature has pity and compassion on horses that this Occurs, for (they say) had this continued to be attached always to the foal, both horses and mares would be inflamed with a passion for uncontrolled mating.

This may, if you like, be a gift bestowed by Poseidon or Athena, the god and the goddess of horses, upon these animals to insure that their race is perpetuated and does not perish through an insane indulgence.

Now those who tend horses are fully aware of this and if they chance to need the aforesaid piece of flesh with the design of kindling the fires of Love in some person, they watch a pregnant Mare, and directly she bears the foal they seize it, cut off the piece of flesh, and deposit it in a Mare's hoof, for there alone will it be securely kept and stored away.

As to the foal, they sacrifice it to the rising sun, for its dam refuses to suckle it any more now that it has lost its birth-token and no longer possesses the premise of her affection. For it is by eating that piece of flesh that the dam begins to love her offspring passionately.

But any man who as a result of some plot tastes of that piece of flesh becomes possessed and consumed by an incontinent desire and cries aloud, and cannot be controlled from going after even the ugliest boys and grown women of repellent aspect.

And he proclaims his affliction and tells those whom he meets how he is being driven mad. And his body pines and wastes away and his mind is agitated by erotic frenzy.

Statue of Mare at Olympia

I have heard also this story of the bronze mare at statue of Olympia: horses fall madly in love with it and long to mount it and at the sight of it neigh amorously.

Hidden away in the charmed bronze it contains the treacherous Mare's-frenzy, and through some secret contrivance of the artist the bronze works against living animals. For it could not possibly be so true to life that horses with their eyes open should be deceived and inflamed to that extent.

It may be that those who relate the, story are speaking the truth, or it may be that they are not:

I have only reported what I have heard.

5. The Sea horse, its poisonous nature

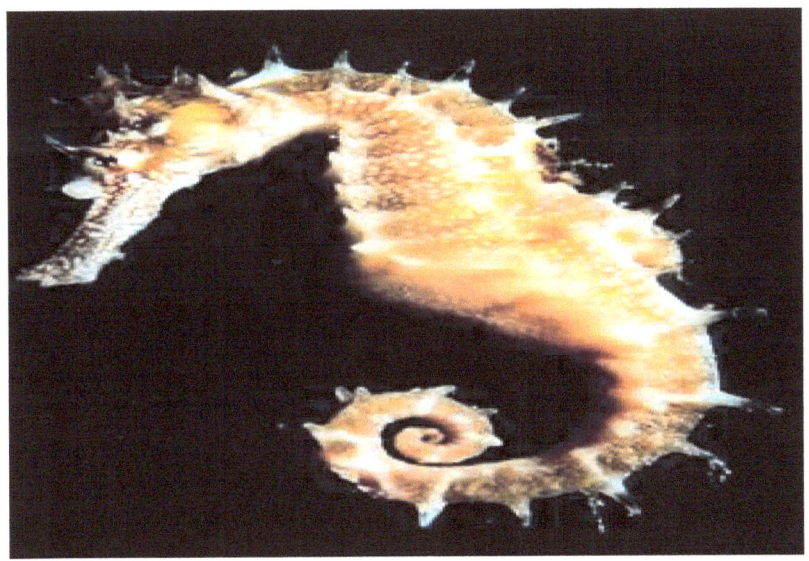

Those who are expert at fishing say that if one boils and dissolves in wine the stomach of the Sea horse and gives it to someone to drink, the wine becomes a poison abnormal in comparison with others.

For the man who has tasted it is first of all seized with a most violent retching; next he is racked with a dry cough but brings up nothing at all; yet his upper stomach is enlarged and swells, while hot streams mount to his head and phlegm descends from his nose, emitting a fishy odour; his eyes turn bloodshot and fiery and the lids become puffy.

He is possessed, they say, by a longing to vomit, but brings up nothing whatever. If however Nature prevails, the man escapes the threat of death but sinks gradually into a state of forgetfulness and insanity. But if the wine penetrates into his lower stomach, it is all over with him, and the victim inevitably dies.

Those who survive, having drifted into insanity, are seized with a strong desire, for water; they yearn to see water and to listen to it falling. This at any rate quiets them and lulls them to sleep. And they like to spend their time either by ever-flowing rivers or near the sea-shore or by the side of springs or lakes, and though they do not at all desire to drink, they love to swim and to dip their feet and to wash their hands.

But there are those who maintain that it is not the actual stomach of the Sea-horse which causes these sufferings, but that the creature feeds upon a certain kind of seaweed of extraordinary bitterness and that its essence is transferred to the Sea-horse. Notwithstanding, the Sea-horse has been found to be an efficient remedy thanks to the shrewdness of an aged fisherman who was versed in matters regarding the sea. There was an old fisherman of Crete and he had some young sons, also fishermen. Now it so happened that the old man caught some Sea-horses along with other fish, and that the boys were bitten by a mad dog: when the first was bitten, the others who came to help him suffered the same fate. So they lay on the beach at Rhithymna in Crete (this is said to be a village), while the spectators sympathised with their plight and gave orders for the dog to be killed and its liver to be given to the boys to eat as an antidote to the poison.

Others urged that they should be taken to the temple of Artemis of Rhocca and that the goddess should be implored to heal them. But the old man, without a sign of fear, without swerving from his purpose, allowed these advisers to make their recommendations, washed out the stomachs of the Sea-horses, some of which he roasted and gave to the boys to apply, while others he pounded into, a mixture of vinegar and honey, and then smeared on the wounds made; by the bite, and so overcame the boys' madness by' that longing for water which the Sea-horses engendered in them. And in this way he cured his sons, though it took time.

6. The otter

I have already said much regarding Dog-fish in the sea. But
river Dog-fish have the appearance of small dogs that live on
land, and they even have hairy, tails.

And it is said that their blood, if poured into a mixture of
water and vinegar, acts as an embrocation for swollen sinews.
Their skin provides excellent shoes, and these too, they say,
are good for the sinews.

The river Tecinus (this is the name of a river in Italy) breeds
the fish called the Grayling, It attains to as much as a cubit in
length, and in appearance is between the basse and the mullet.
The odour of the fish when caught is something to astonish
one, for it is not the least like the fishy odour of others, but
you would say that you held in your hand some freshly
plucked thyme; moreover it is sweet-scented and a man who
did not notice the fish would fancy that the herb which is the
bees' principal food (from which incidentally the fish
thymallus, derives its name) was in your hand.

How Caught

The easiest way to catch it is with a net; with a how caught lure and hook you will not catch it, neither with; hog's fat nor with a gnat nor with a clam nor with the entrails of any other fish nor with the muscle of a spiral-shell. It is only to be caught with a mosquito, a troublesome insect, man's enemy by day and by night with its sting and its buzzing: that will catch the aforesaid Grayling, for this is the only bait that it delights in.

7. The sword fish

These last are suited to their name, witness the fact that the rest of their body is soft and harmless to the touch, that their teeth do not appear curved and sharp, that there are no spines springing erect from their back, as in the case of dolphins, or from their tail.

But what surprises one to learn and to see is this: the jaw just below its nose, through which it breathes arid through which the stream flows to the gills and falls out, is prolonged to a. sharp point, is straight and increases gradually in length and in bulk; it grows also as the fish grows into a monster and resembles the beak of a trireme.

And the Sword-fish makes straight for fishes, kills them, and then feeds on them, and with this same sword beats off the attacks of the largest sea- monsters. No smith has forged this weapon which grows upon the fish, and Nature has made it sharp.

And so when these Sword-fish have attained a considerable size they even attack ships. And there are some who boast that they have seen a Bithynian vessel drawn up on shore in order that the keel which was suffering from, age might receive the necessary attention, and fixed to the keel they saw the head of a sword-fish.

For the creature had planted the sword given it by Nature, in the vessel, and when it attempted to withdraw, the whole of its body was rent from the neck owing to the force of the ship s onrush, while the sword remained fixed just as it entered originally. So then this fish is caught both in the sea arid in the Ister, and it delights both in salt water and in fresh streams.

8. A deadly Seaweed

When the summer is at its hottest, Sharks and other fish which are bold by nature approach the sea-shore and make straight for cliffs and run in under headlands where the current is strong and swim into narrow, deep straits.

They forsake their haunts in the open seas and at this season neglect their feeding-ground there.. Now a certain seaweed grows among, deep reefs: it is about the size of a tamarisk and bears fruit resembling a poppy.

At other seasons of the year the fruit is closed and is resistant and hard like a shell it opens however this has not been identified, but there is no known sea- weed that is poisonous to fish, and much of Aelian's description appears to be fanciful after the summer solstice, like buds in rose-gardens. And the, surrounding sheath protects the inside, encircling it like a barrier: it is a bright yellow colour, but the part beneath this covering is dark blue and flabby like a bladder with air in it, and is quite translucent; arid from it there oozes a violent poison.

By night this seaweed sends out a fiery ray and sparkles. And when the Dog-star is raising the evil power of the poison is even stronger. For that reason all fishermen have given it the name of Pancynium in the belief that it is the rising of the star that generates the poison.

Now the Sharks fall upon the flower which by night seems to be burning, rushing at this tamarisk of the sea as if it were treasure trove, and when the poison has drenched them, some being swallowed and some having penetrated through their gills, they die and at once float up tq the surface.

Now those who are skilled at investigating such matters collect this poison which emanates from the aforesaid monsters, some of it from other parts of the creature's body and some from its mouth; This poison is second only to that of the land-peony, as it is called, which people have also named Cynospastus, The reason for this you will learn if I remember to tell it you.

9. The Moesians and their fishing

The people of Mysia not those who inhabit the Pergamum of
Telephus, but you are to understand those who live by the
Black Sea in the lower part and are neighbors of the Scythians
whose inroads they check, and who are guardians of the
aforesaid country on behalf of Rome.
I am referring; to those that live near Heraclea and the river
Axius. It is there, you know, that the inhabitants tell the tale of
Medea, daughter of Aeetes, whose impious hands dared to
commit that outrage upon her brother Apsyrtus, for the
Mysians harp on this evil report against the Colchian
sorceress, besides the others that are current among the
Greeks.

Well, this is the way in which these people hunt fish. An Istrian whose trade is fishing drives a pair of oxen near the bank of the Ister, but not because he has the least wish to plough, for, as the saying goes, an ox and a dolphin have nothing in common; so in the same way what friendship can there be between a fisherman's hands and a plough?

If however he has a pair of horses he uses horses. The man carries the yoke on his shoulders and comes to a spot where he thinks it suitable to sit down and where he believes he is well placed for fishing. One end of his, rope, which is stout and thoroughly capable of standing a strain, he attaches to the middle of the yoke.

The Sheat-fish

He provides ample fodder for the oxen or the horses, and they eat their fill. And to the other end of the .rope he attaches a strong hook which has been well sharpened, and on this he spits the lungs of a bull, and lets them down as food, and indeed its favourite food, for the Sheat-fish in the Ister, after the fastening above the point where the rope secures the hook enough lead to prevent it from being dragged away.

So directly the fish notices the bull's meat he rushes to seize it. Then, finding what he wants, all at once with jaws agape he recklessly tugs at the deadly meal which has come to him.. Next, this glutton, drawn on by his enjoyment, is spitted on the aforesaid hook before he knows it, and in his eagerness to escape the disaster that has befallen him he agitates and shakes the rope with all his might.

So when the hunter is aware of this he is filled with joy; he leaps from his seat, abandons his labours in the river and his watery pursuits, and like-actor in a play changing his mask, sets his pair of oxen or horses in motion, and there ensues a trial of strength between the monster and the beasts of burden.

For the creature bred in the Ister exerts a downward pull with all the strength at his command, while the pair of beasts pulling in the opposite direction makes the rope taut. But it avails the fish nothing: at any rate he is defeated in the tug-of-war, gives up, and is hauled ashore. A student of Homer might say that mules were hauling tree- trunks, as Homer sings in the celebrated tale of the funeral of Patroclus.

The Ister in winter

There is also in the Ister a bay of immense depth and like the sea in its wide compass. More- over that this bay attains a considerable depth is sufficiently proved by the following fact: merchant vessels which cross the sea put in to this bay and, when the bay is angered by the winds that blow and lash it into waves and drive it mad, are just as afraid of it as they are of the sea.

And there are also islands in it, and even creeks along the shore into which one can run. for safety There are besides, promontories and capes running out, on which the waves in their fury dash and burst whenever the river at its very fullest is, as it were, forced into a narrow space as it presses on to the sea.

This commonly occurs when the third, autumnal season is past and the winter season is setting in and the river is running in full flood. And as it rises the north wind urges it forward and causes it to descend in fury.

And the stream carries down the ice it contains as though for an easy voyage But the north wind opposes it with its violent and icy blasts it does riot permit it to discharge into the sea what you might call its offspring, but causes it to overflow, resists it, and brings it to a halt.

So the ice which is floating and checked sinks and solidifies to .a great depth. In consequence the Ister's own water flows beneath, along what you might call hidden channels, while the newly acquired and alien surface resembles a plain, and at this season of the year the people thereabouts travel along it driving a pair or on horseback.

Now the way in which that mischievous and crafty animal the fox tests and examines this river and the Strymon in Thrace to see if they are frozen, I have described earlier on.

10. Ships ice-bound

Well, the ice on the Ister freezes hard even round a merchant
vessel on its way downstream and imprisons it: it is no use to
spread the sails; the man at the prow looks no more ahead; the
ship's captain cannot move the rudders to and fro; they are
fixed fast, for the whole vessel is caught in the surrounding
fetters and looks,
I declare, not like any ship, for it is no longer beaten by the
waves, but like some hill rising from a wide expanse of plain
or for the entire world like some lofty watch-tower.
Thereupon the passengers and the sailors jump out and hurry
down the river and fetch wagons and transfer the cargo on to
what was lately the water.
Then again when the winter season is over and the river
begins to flow strongly they still carry their loads. But the ship
remains stationary until the frost relaxes and the ice melts and
is dissolved, and the merchant vessel, freed from its strange
cable, is released.

11. Fishing in winter

At that season fishermen also take picks and hack Fishing in through the ice wherever they feel inclined, and contrive a circular hole reaching down to the water. You would say that it was the mouth of a well or of a huge, very pot-bellied jar. Thereupon multitudes of fish wishing to escape from the ice which is pressing down upon them like a roof, and longing for the light, swim joyfully up to the opening that has been made, and come in crowds past numbering and jostle one another, and being in a confined hole are easily captured.

And it is possible to catch carp and crow- fish in abundance and perch and the swordfish, though the last-named is not yet fully grown and is still without the frontal spike; sturgeon too, young and tender, for the large ones of mature age may be the size of the biggest Tunny.

12. The Sturgeon

The Sturgeon is extremely fat along the; sides and the belly; you might say they were the dugs of a sow that was suckling its young. It has a rough skin and spear- makers actually polish their spear-shafts on it. Beneath the spinal marrow of this creature a supple, narrow membrane beginning at the middle of the head, runs down as far as the tail.

Now if you let this dry in the sun you will obtain, should you wish it, a whip to drive a pair of horses with. For it differs hardly at all from a leather thong. When however the fish has grown to its full size one would not see it emerging from the ice and falling into the hole, but either .it slips beneath some all-sheltering rock or buries itself in deep sand and is only too glad to keep warm.

And at that time it needs no vegetation, no other fish to eat, but prefers to remain inactive while the frost lasts, and is happy to be idle and consumes its own fat, just as octopuses also when unable to catch any prey nibble their own tentacles and feed off themselves.

But when winter is over and spring is beginning and the Ister is flowing freely, it hates to be inactive and, swimming up to the surface, takes its fill of the foam on the water, and there is foam in abundance as the stream roars and boils in violent, tumult.

Then is the time when it is easily captured as the fishermen lie in wait for it and let down hook and line into the foam. The whiteness of the foam conceals the hook and the bright sheen of the bronze is invisible to the fish; hence, as it opens its jaws and takes a heavy draught of the aforesaid food, it swallows the bait and meets its death from the very thing that before sustained it.

13. The Peony, how plucked

There is a plant of the name of *Cynospastus* (it is also called *Aglaopkotis* (peony): I have remembered and wish to fulfill my obligations) which by daytime passes unnoticed among the rest and is hardly visible, bait at night it becomes visible arid shines but like a star, for it is of a fiery nature and like a flame. Therefore men plant some mark near the roots and then go away, for if they did not do this they would be unable by day to remember either the colour or even the appearance of the plant.

But when the night is over they come and see the mark which they left and recognise, it and are able to guess that this is the very plant that they need; for otherwise it is completely like the plants all round it, differing from them not one whit.

But they themselves do not pull up this plant; if they did they would certainly regret it. Accordingly no one either digs round it or pulls it up, for (they say) the first man who in ignorance of its nature touched it, was destroyed by it shortly afterwards.

And so they bring a strong dog that has not been fed for some days and is ravenously hungry and attach a strong cord to it, and round the stalk of the Peony at the bottom they fasten a noose securely from as far away as they can; then they put before the dog a large quantity of cooked meat which exhales a savoury odour.

And the dog, burning with hunger and tormented by the savour, rushes at the meat that has been placed before it and with its violent movement pulls up the plant, roots and all. But when the sun sees the roots the dog immediately dies, arid they bury it on the spot, and after performing some mysterious rites arid paying honour to the dead body of the dog as having died on their behalf, they then make bold to touch the aforesaid plant and carry it home.

It is useful, they say, for many purposes; for instance, it is said to cure the disease with which the moon is reputed to afflict men; also that affliction of the eyes in which moisture floods them and then congeals and- so robs them of their sight.

14. The Nerites: two myths

There is in the sea a shellfish with a spiral shell, small in size but of surpassing beauty, and it is born where the water is at its purest and upon rocks beneath the sea and on what are called sunken reefs. Its name is *Nerites* two stories are in circulation touching this creature, and both have reached me; moreover the telling of a short tale in the middle of a lengthy history is simply giving the hearer a rest and sweetening the narrative.

Hesiod sings of how Doris the daughter of Oceanus bore fifty daughters to Nereus the sea-god, whom to this day we always hear of as truthful and unlying. Homer also mentions them in his poems. But they do not state that one son was born after all that number of daughters, though he is celebrated in mariner's tales.

And they say that he was named Nerites and was the most beautiful of men and. gods; also that Aphrodite delighted to be with Nerites in the sea and loved him. And when the fated time arrived, at which, at the bidding of the Father of the gods, Aphrodite, also had to be enrolled among the Olympians, I have heard that she ascended and wished to bring her companion and play-fellow.

But the story goes that he refused, preferring life with his sisters and parents to Olympus. And then he was permitted to grow wings: this, I imagine was a gift from Aphrodite. But even this favour he counted as nothing.

And so the daughter of Zeus was moved to anger and transformed his shape into this shell and of her own accord chose in his place for her attendant and servant Eros, who also was young and beautiful, and to him she gave the wings, of Nerites.

But the other account proclaims that Poseidon was the lover of Nerites, and that Nerites returned his love, and that this was the origin of the celebrated Anteros (mutual love).

And so, as I am told, for the rest the favourite spent his time with his lover, and moreover when Poseidon drove his chariot over the waves, all other great fishes as well as dolphins and tritons too, sprang up from their deep haunts and gamboled and danced around the chariot, only to be left utterly and far behind by the speed of his horses; only the boy favourite was his escort close at hand.

And before them the waves sank to rest and the sea: parted out of reverence to Poseidon, for the god willed that his beautiful favourite should not only be highly esteemed for other reasons but should also be pre-eminent at swimming. But the story relates that the Sun resented the boy's power of speed and transformed his body into the spiral shell as it now is: the cause of his anger I cannot tell, neither does the fable mention it. But if one may guess where there is nothing to go by, Poseidon and the Sun might be said to be rivals.

And it may be that the Sun was vexed at the boy travelling about in the sea and wished that he should travel among the constellations instead of being counted among sea-monsters. Thus far the two fables; but may the gods be good to me, and for my part let me observe a religious silence regarding them. But if my fables have said anything overbold, the fault must be laid to their charge.

15. Winter Fishing in the Eridanus

At the spot where the Tanarus and the Eridanus meet (the, latter has achieved renown and fame, whereas the former is hardly known at all) an altogether peculiar manner of fishing is in vogue;, it has come to my knowledge through the poems of a mail of Mytilene, an acquaintance of my own, and must not pass without a tribute in my narrative.

When the rivers have become ice-bound those who live in their neighborhood plough and sow in the winter season, for it is their lot to possess a fertile land. Then at the beginning of spring while the aforesaid rivers are still immobile for the reason that I explained, the erstwhile farmers now fishermen select some spot like a bay and with well- sharpened hatchets cut round it so that a circle of water, like a pond, appears. They do not however cut close to the bank as yet but leave the ice as it froze originally. So then they throw a wide net round the space which they have laid open, and round the net a stoutish rope. This net is drawn in by men standing on the shore, fishermen and others, and there are many who though they know nothing of the art, watch the fish being caught: they feel a certain fascination in it.

But as the men are drawn in and approach the bank, then the fishermen on the dry land cut the ice there also, for they have an interest in the capture and try to prevent the fish from escaping. When this has been done as described, the net, full of fish, pushes the block of ice that has been cut round and draws it along with it, while the fishermen who are standing on the block look as if they were being carried along on a floating island.

Such is the peculiar method of catching the fish there and quite unlike any other. And Homer will allow me to say that these men earn a double wage, one from the river and another from the land, since the same men are both mariners and farmers.

16. Fly-fishing in Macedonia

I have heard and can tell of a way of catching fish in Macedonia, and it is this. Between Beroea and Thessalonica there flows a river called the Astraeus. Now there are in it fishes of a speckled hue, but what the natives call them, it is better to enquire of the Macedonians.

Now these fish feed upon the flies of the country which flit about the river and which are quite unlike flies elsewhere; they do not look like wasps, nor could one fairly describe this creature as comparable in shape with what are called *Anthedones* (bumble-bees), nor even with actual honey-bees, although they possess a distinctive feature of each of the aforesaid insects.

Thus, they have the audacity of the fly; you might say they are the size of a bumble-bee, but their colour imitates that of a wasp, and they buzz like a honeybee. All the natives call them *Hippurus*.

These flies settle on the stream and seek the food that they like; they cannot however escape the observation of the fishes that swim below. So when a fish observes a Hippurus on the surface it swims up noiselessly under water for fear of disturbing the surface and to avoid scaring its prey.

Then when close at hand in the fly s shadow it opens its jaws and swallows the fly, just as a wolf snatches a sheep from the flock, or as an eagle seizes a goose from the farmyard. Having done this it plunges beneath the ripple.

Now although fishermen know of these happenings, they do not in fact make any use of these flies as baits for fish, because if the human hand touches them it destroys the natural bloom; their wings wither and the fish refuse to eat them, and for that reason will not go near them, because by some mysterious instinct they detest flies that have been caught.

And so with the skill of anglers the men circumvent the fish by the following artful contrivance. They wrap the hook in scarlet wool, and to the wool they attach two feathers that grow beneath a cock's wattles and are the colour of wax. The fishing-rod is six feet long, and so is the line.

So they let down this lure, and the fish attracted and excited by the colour, comes to meet it, and fancying from the beauty of the sight that he is going to have a wonderful banquet, opens wide his mouth, is entangled with the hook, and gains a bitter feast, for he is caught.

17. The Ram-Fish

Ram-fishes, whose name has a wide circulation, although information about them is not very definite except in so far as displayed in works of art, spend the winter near the strait between Corsica and Sardinia and actually appear above water.

And round about them, swim dolphins of very great size; Now the male Ram-fish has a white band running round its forehead (you might describe it as the tiara of a Lysimachus or an Antigonus or of some other king of Macedon), but the female has curls, just as cocks have wattles, attached below its neck.

Male and female alike pounce upon dead bodies and feed on them, indeed they even seize living men, and with the wave caused by their swimming, since they are large and of immense bulk, they even overturn vessels, such a storm do they unaided raise against them. And they even snatch men standing on the shore close at hand.

The inhabitants of Corsica tell how, when a ship was wrecked in a storm, a man who was a very strong swimmer managed to swim over a wide, expanse of sea and to secure a hold on some headland in their country; he climbed out and stood there, all fear banished, for he was now free from all perils, with no anxiety for his life, his own master.

Now a Ram-fish which was swimming by caught sight of him as he stood, and inflamed with hunger turned about, arched its back, and with its tail drove a great mass of water forward, and then rose as the swelling wave lifted it, and in a moment was carried up on to the headland and like a hurricane or whirlwind seized the man. So much for the Ram- fish's prey ravished off Corsica.

Those who live on the shores of Ocean tell a fable of how the ancient kings of Atlantis sprung from, the seed of Poseidon, wore upon their head the bands from the male Ram-fish, as an emblem of their authority, while their wives, the queens, wore the curls of the females as a proof of theirs.

Now this creature has exceedingly powerful nostrils and inhales a great quantity of breath, drawing to itself an immense amount of air; and it hunts seals in the following manner. Directly the seals realise that a Ram-fish is somewhere close at hand, bringing destruction upon them, they swim ashore with all possible speed and pass over the land and plunge into the shelter of rocky caverns.

But the Ram- fish perceive that they have fled and give chase, and as they face the cave they know from the smell of flesh that their prey is within, and, as though by some all-powerful spell, with their nostrils they draw in the air that intervenes between themselves and the seal.

But the seal avoids the attack of the monster's breath, as it might an arrow or a spear- point, and at first withdraws, but is finally dragged out of the cave by the overmastering pull and follows against its will, just as though it were bound fast with thongs or cords, and shrieking provides the Ram-fish with a meal.

Those who are skilled at exploring these matters assert that the hairs which grow, from the nostrils of the Ram-fish serve many purposes.

18. The Tunny

In the gulf of Vibo there are shoals of Tunny past numbering, and some are, like hogs, solitary, and swim by themselves and are of very great size; others swim in couples or range together, as wolves do; others again swim in companies, just like herds of goats, ranging over wide feeding-grounds.
But at the rising of the Dog-star and when the sun's rays are at their fiercest, they set out for the Euxine. And if the waves seem hot to them they swim interwoven with one another and by the contact of their bodies somehow contrive to get a certain amount of shade

19. The 'Moon-fish'

Demostratus, a man deeply versed in fishing lore and excellent at expounding it, says that there is a certain fish of great beauty and that it is called the ' Moon-fish'; it is small, dark blue in colour, and flat in shape. He says too that it has dorsal fins which it raises, but that they are soft and neither unyielding nor rough.

These fins, whenever the fish dives, open out and form & half-circle and present to the eye the shape of a half-moon. This is what the fishermen of Cyprus say, but Demostratus adds that if this fish is caught when the moon is at the full, it too is at the full, and causes trees to expand if one brings it and attaches it to them.

But when the moon is waning the fish pines and dies, and if applied to plants they too wither. And when wells are being dug, if, as the moon is waxing, you throw this fish into the water which you have found, it will flow continually and never fail; if however you do this when the moon is waning, the flow will cease.

In the same way if you throw this same fish into a bubbling spring, you will henceforward either find it full of water or you will find the spot empty.

20. Tunny Fishing in the Euxine

I know that I have somewhere earlier on in this discourse described how Tunny swim into and out of the Propontis. Just consider the cities along the Black Sea-Heraclea, Tium and Amastris.

Now the inhabitants of the whole of that country know exactly of the coming of the Tunny, and at that season of the year the fish arrive, and much gear has been got ready to deal with them, boats and nets and a high lookout-place.

This lookout-place is fixed on some beach and stands where there is a wide, uninterrupted view. It is no trouble to me to explain, and you who listen should be pleased to hear, how it is constructed. Two high pine-trunks held apart by wide balks of timber, are set up ; the latter are interwoven in the structure at short intervals and are of great assistance to the watchman in mounting to the top.

Each of the boats has six young men, strong rowers, on either side. The nets are of considerable length; they are not too light and so far from being kept floating by corks are actually weighted with lead, and these fish swim into them in shoals. And when the spring begins to shine and the breezes are blowing softly and the air is bright and as it were smiling and the waves are at rest and the sea smooth, the watcher, whose mysterious skill and naturally sharp sight enable him to see the fish, announces to the fishermen the quarter from which they are coming: if on the one hand the men ought to spread their nets near the shore, he instructs them accordingly ; but if closer in, like a-general he gives the signal, or like a conductor, the keynote.

And frequently he will tell the total number of fish .and not be off the mark. And, this is what happens. When the company of Tunnies makes for the open sea, the man in the lookout who has an accurate knowledge of their ways shouts at the top of his voice telling the men to give chase in that direction and to row straight for the open sea.

And the men after fastening to one of the pines supporting the lookout a very long rope attached to the nets,, then proceed to row their boats in close order and in column, keeping near to one another, because, you see, the net is distributed between each, boat.

And the first boat drops its portion of the net and turns back; then the second does the same, then the third, and the fourth has to let go its portion. But the rowers in the fifth boat delay, for they must not let go yet.

Then the others row in different directions and haul their part of the net, and then pause. Now the Tunny are sluggish and incapable of any action that involves daring, arid they remain huddled together and quite still.

So the rowers, as though it were a captured city, take captive—as a poet might say—the population of fishes. And so, my Grecian friends, the people of Eretria and Naxos know of these things by report, for they have learnt about this method of fishing all that Herodotus and others relate. What remains to be told of it you shall learn from others.

Tunny fishers and Poseidon

When Tunny have been caught by fishermen of the Euxine (and I might, add off Sicily also, for what else had Sophron in mind when he wrote his delightful *Tunny-fisher*. Anyhow there are Tunny- fisheries in other places besides.)—when therefore they are safely enmeshed in the net, then' is the time when everybody prays to Poseidon the Averter of Disaster.

And as I ask myself the reason, I think it worthwhile to explain what induced them to attach the name 'Averter of Disaster' to the god. They pray to the brother of Zeus, the Lord of the Sea, that neither swordfish nor dolphin may come as fellow-traveler with the shoal of Tunny.

At any rate your noble sword-fish has many a time cut through the net and allowed the whole company to break through and go free. The dolphin also is the net's, enemy, for it is, skilful at gnawing its way out.

21. Pearl-fishing in the Indian Ocean

The Pearl-oyster of India; (I have spoken earlier on of the one in the Red Sea) is obtained in the following manner. There is a, city of which one Ocean Soras by name was ruler, a man of royal, lineage, at the time when Eucratides was ruler of Bactria. And the name of the city is Ferimula, and it is inhabited by Ichthyophagi (fish-eaters).

These men, it is said, set out from there with their nets and draw a ring of wide embrace round a great circle of the shore. The aforesaid stone is produced from a shell resembling a large trumpet-shell, and the Pearl- oysters swim in shoals and have leaders, just as bees, in their hives have kings, as they are called.

And I have heard that the 'leader' too is conspicuous for his colour and his size. Now divers beneath the waters make it their special aim to capture him, for once he is caught they catch the entire shoal, since it is, so to say, left destitute and without a leader; for it remains motionless and ceases to advance, like a flock of sheep that by some mischance has lost its shepherd.

But the leader makes good his escape and slips out with the utmost adroitness and takes the lead and rescues those that obey him. Those however those are caught the Ichthyophagi are said to pickle in jars.

And when the flesh turns clammy and falls away, the precious stone is left behind. The best ones are those from India and from the Red Sea; but they are also found in the western ocean where the island of Britain is, though this kind has a more golden appearance, and a duller, duskier sheen.

Juba asserts that they occur also in the strait leading to the Bosporus and are inferior to the British kind, and are not for a moment to be compared with those from India and the Red Sea.

But the land-pearl of India is said not to have an independent origin but to be generated not from the ice formed by frost but from excavated rock-crystal.

Get All The Books In The Series:

Animal Peculiarity Volume 1 Part [1-8]
Animal Peculiarity Volume 2 Part [1-8]
Animal Peculiarity Volume 3 Part [1-8]

www.ingramcontent.com/pod-product-compliance
Lightning Source LLC
Chambersburg PA
CBHW050844290526
45792CB00002B/510